The Business
of Cybersecurity

The Business of Cybersecurity

Foundations and Ideologies

Ashwini Sathnur

 BUSINESS EXPERT PRESS

The Business of Cybersecurity: Foundations and Ideologies
Copyright © Business Expert Press, LLC, 2019.

As part of the Business Law Collection, this book discusses general principles of law for the benefit of the public through education only. This book does not undertake to give individual legal advice. Nothing in this book should be interpreted as creating an attorney-client relationship with the author(s). The discussions of legal frameworks and legal issues is not intended to persuade readers to adopt general solutions to general problems, but rather simply to inform readers about the issues. Readers should not rely on the contents herein as a substitute for legal counsel. For specific advice about legal issues facing you, consult with a licensed attorney.

First published in 2019 by
Business Expert Press, LLC
222 East 46th Street, New York, NY 10017
www.businessexpertpress.com

ISBN-13: 978-1-94897-618-3 (paperback)
ISBN-13: 978-1-94897-619-0 (e-book)

Business Expert Press Business Law and Corporate Risk Management Collection

Collection ISSN: 2333-6722 (print)
Collection ISSN: 2333-6730 (electronic)

Cover and interior design by S4Carlisle Publishing Services Private Ltd., Chennai, India

First edition: 2019

10 9 8 7 6 5 4 3 2 1

Printed in the United States of America.

Abstract

Cybersecurity could be defined as beginning of the concept of trust and belief in cyber transactions. The era of computing began in the 20th century, with an enormous investment on computational research. Software programming languages were the foundational blocks of history of computing. Progressive research then led to networking, bringing about the formation of connectivity. Along with these creations, there was an accompanying factor of compromise on data privacy and hacking of data. This factor was the introduction to cybersecurity.

This book is primarily created for the objective of knowledge sharing and knowledge-enabling on the conceptual ideologies of the cybersecurity. This book is aimed at students, early-career researchers, and also advanced researchers and professionals. The case studies described in the book create renewed knowledge on the innovations built on the applied theories of cybersecurity. These case studies focus on the financial markets and space technologies.

Keywords

cybersecurity; trust; information and communication technologies; hacking; digital financial services; digital fiat currency; blockchain; financial inclusion; accessibility; innovation

Contents

Acknowledgments

I thank the publishers and printers of this book for providing a platform for communicating and marketing this work, embodying detailed descriptions and definitions of the latest frontiers of the emerging technologies and conceptual ideologies and frameworks.

I also thank the International Telecommunications Union for providing me with the platform of the focus group of Digital Financial Services, which facilitated my research on the payments systems and gave me the opportunity to create this research report, included in this book.

Finally, I thank Business Expert Press for this opportunity to disseminate information on the latest frontiers of technology and conceptual ideologies, reflecting the latest trend in the market.

Thank you, readers!

CHAPTER 1

Introduction to Cybersecurity

Cybersecurity could be defined as "Beginning of the concept of trust and belief in cyber transactions." The era of computing began in the twentieth century, with an enormous investment in computational research. Software programming languages were the foundational blocks of history of computing. Progressive research then led to more extensive networking, bringing about the formation of connectivity. Along with these technological developments emerged the issues of breach of data privacy and data hacking. These factors along with the explosive growth in Internet-driven commerce paved the way for the emergence of cybersecurity as study field of paramount significance.

Both research groups and individual researchers were working toward developing robust cybersecurity tools and technologies.

When internetworking arose, individuals could capture the data that were being transferred. The concept of hacking can be explained this way: When a physical, package mail is posted from Bangalore to Mysore, it could be easy for an intruder to access it and view its contents. Similarly, data transmitted from machine A to machine B over a technological medium—while on its journey—could be picked up by another machine/individual/groups of individuals. Due to this reason, cybersecurity has become vital for the safety and security of the data. Thus, cybersecurity is fundamentally about thwarting any bid from criminal entities such as hackers who try to illegally access and steal data that are stored in servers, or in cloud, and are transmitted electronically or via the Internet.

During the earlier phases of computer technology and research, the technology of cybersecurity first emerged in the form of a computer program that was built to thwart any intruders from breaching and gaining entry into the computer systems to access and steal data. The software languages that were existent were used to build and execute software programs that provided cybersecurity.

The first computer software language that explained much of the fundamentals of computing was BASIC. Thus, anti-hacking modules were written first in BASIC language.

Algorithm for cybersecurity in BASIC:-

```
LET AFLAG = 0
IF NETWORK != "Connected"
THEN
   AFLAG = 0
ELSE
   # Data transmission
   NETWORK = "Connected"
   # Send data over network
   WHILE "Data transfer"
      IF personA.hackedData() = true
      THEN
         AFLAG = 1
      ENDIF
   END WHILE
END IF
IF #AFLAG = 1
THEN
   Hacking Data
   Cybersecurity module invoked
ENDIF
```

CHAPTER 2

Theory of Cybersecurity

As described in the previous chapter, innovative ideologies of algorithms were developed and introduced in cybersecurity concepts. The theory of cybersecurity rests wholly on the ideologies of computing research. Programming languages are utilized for building cybersecurity modules.

Fundamentally, cybersecurity programs are written in programming languages such as BASIC, C, C++, and Java. Algorithm is first designed and written. In the next step, a functional design flowchart is drawn based on the algorithm written in the first step. In the third, and final, step, codes are written in the software language chosen to create cybersecurity modules and programs as shown in Figure 2.1.

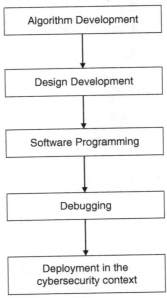

Figure 2.1 Functional design flowchart

Modules of programming for cybersecurity are listed as follows:

A) BASIC
B) C
C) C++
D) Java

Data structure is a component of the software language program that defines the constituent data members and the methods that process these data members (Figure 2.2).

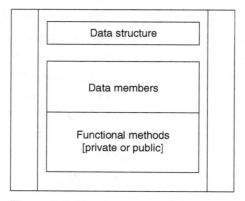

Figure 2.2 Data structure of the components

Data Members

These are constituents of the variety of data contained within a cyber-security functionality.

Functional Methods

These are constituents of the variety of functions and methods used for operating the data members—basically they provide the requirements and functionalities of the cybersecurity module.

Program Contribution to Data Structure

BASIC, C, C++, Java are some of the program languages used for writing codes to be used for executing cybersecurity modules.

The theories of cybersecurity are founded on the concept of fraud. Data theft is common in networking. Hacking and compromise of security are frequently encountered.

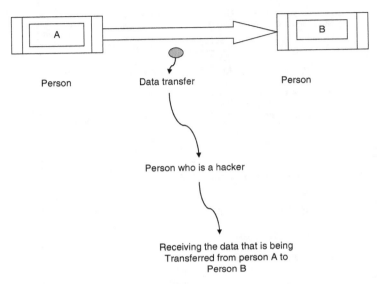

Figure 2.3 Fraud detection

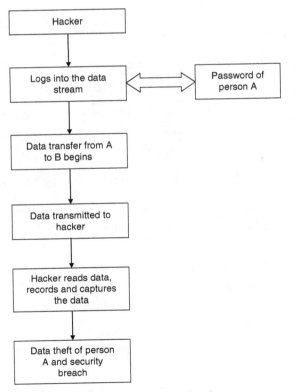

Figure 2.4 Methodology of the hacker

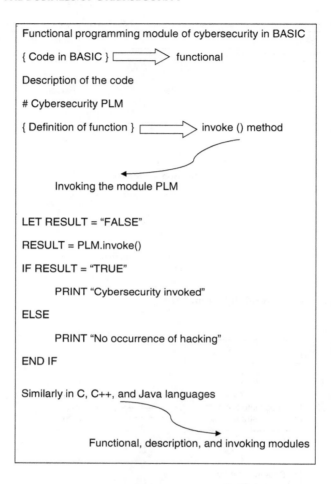

Functional programming module of cybersecurity in BASIC

{ Code in BASIC } ⟹ functional

Description of the code

Cybersecurity PLM

{ Definition of function } ⟹ invoke () method

Invoking the module PLM

LET RESULT = "FALSE"

RESULT = PLM.invoke()

IF RESULT = "TRUE"

     PRINT "Cybersecurity invoked"

ELSE

     PRINT "No occurrence of hacking"

END IF

Similarly in C, C++, and Java languages

Functional, description, and invoking modules

Database Design of the Cybersecurity Module

The database design involves creating the following components that are as essential and integral part of cybersecurity modules.

A) Database data constituents for storage of content to be protected by cybersecurity programs
B) Database data constituents that are structural elements in the cyber-security module
C) Database data constituents that invoke member applications

The various methods of the functioning of database is defined.

First, the method to add data to the database is defined, which is DBMSAdd() function.

Second, the database function method "delete" is defined. This function removes data from the database—DBMSRemoveSelectedOrAll().

Third, the database function method to search for certain data is defined DBMSFindByColumn().

Then these three functions are defined in the software languages BASIC, C, C++, and Java.

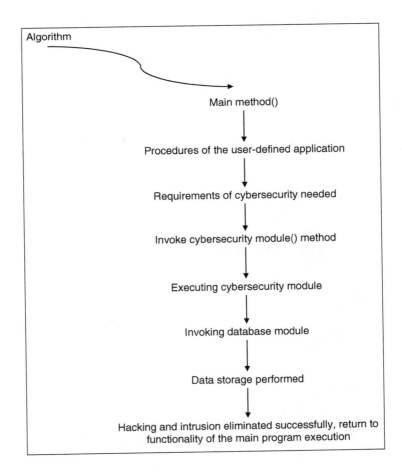

CHAPTER 3

Emerging Technologies for the Theories of Cybersecurity

Rigorous research has been taking place in the field of information and communication technology (ICT) to develop and provide newer methodologies and procedures for use in cybersecurity modules. Thus, new cybersecurity modules have been emerging even more frequently than in the earlier times, given the exponential rise in the growth of data corresponding to a staggering increase in the use of Internet that has permeated all aspects of our life: technological, commercial, social, and personal. Then arises the question: Who are the individuals and institutions that are in most need of these modular scriptures of cybersecurity?

Those who are affected by data theft and are victims of breach of cyber privacy are general users of cybersecurity programs. The affected could be individuals or community groups or organizations. The sectors that are mainly using and transmitting highly sensitive and valuable commercial data—such as online banking, digital financial services, and digital fiat currency—are important users of cybersecurity programs.

Blockchain technology Figure 3.1, crypto currencies, and data protection programs in space science are some basic examples of fields that actively use cybersecurity modules. Any infrastructure requirement for sectors such as space science is primarily supplied by governments. The needs of private sectors for space devices and equipment are also satisfied by provisions made by the public sector and government organizations. Thus, there is a mandate for the flow of resources from the public to the private sectors. An agreement, or a form of relationship or association, is created between the public and the private sectors. This arrangement or consortium is called the public–private partnership. Space science tools are resources used by private networks, which could include individuals or organizations whose work is carried out through public-private partnerships. The theories of cybersecurity, as mentioned previously, require awareness building. Resources such as books, online materials, e-learnings, and webinars are the means that facilitate knowledge-building in the field of cybersecurity.

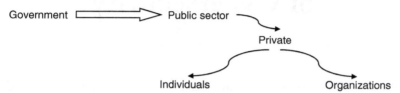

Figure 3.1 Blockchain technology methodology

CHAPTER 4

Innovative Ideologies of the Theories of Blockchain Technologies

Blockchain originated in the conceptual framework of the digital financial services and financial inclusion. The origin of digital financial inclusion gives rise to the requirements of advanced concepts of cybersecurity. General Data Protection Regulation (GPDR) is the latest framework of cybersecurity in the European Union.

These ideologies, theories, and practices could be transferred to the people from the originating context. Knowledge transfers are mandatory. What are the mechanisms utilized for this transfer?

A) Publication of books
B) Dissemination of research articles published in the international platform
C) Knowledge-providing websites
D) Content management of the information
E) Communications on latest information
F) Creation of policies

Once knowledge transfer happens, the required knowledge becomes available for public consumption. Then comes the situation where there is a requirement for society and organizations to create products and business concepts revolving around the ideologies of cybersecurity.

Upon imbibing the procedures, organizations create product/project proposals and innovations spanning across the various theories of cybersecurity.

Upon creating an agreement on these ideas and projects, implementation of these technological products in cybersecurity is executed. This implementation follows a sequence of processes and steps leading to the successful manufacturing of the end-product.

During the processes of product building, separate teams are formed for the implementation of the product being developed.

Product implementation follows the software development lifecycle (SDLC) in Figure 4.1.

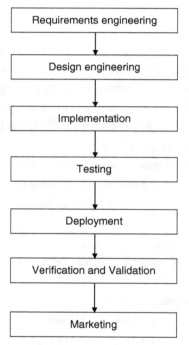

Figure 4.1 SDLC life cycle

Later, a user manual is written to help guide customers in using the software program. A guiding inference information, usually in the form of a booklet capturing all the basic requirements for customers' use and benefit, is provided to the end-users.

For the manufacture of the product, various departments come into focus. Various departments coordinate and work with product department to carry out the following key functions:

A) Testing
B) Verification and validation
C) Design
D) Launch
E) Marketing

Based on innovations, any reforms in the afore-mentioned processes can be managed. Reforms in the cybersecurity division have created solutions that have led to an industrial revolution.

CHAPTER 5

ICTs Introduced into the Applications of the Concept of Digital Financial Services and Financial Inclusion

The rapid technological advancement in the field information and communication technology (ICT) has created enormous employment opportunities in cybersecurity. Cybersecurity is the core concept in multiple innovations and sectors. For example, digital financial services such as blockchain totally relies on cybersecurity technologies for its objective of consumer protection.

Strategies adopted for financial inclusion requires cybersecurity at the level of development ideologies, as cybersecurity is at the core of financial services.

Certain technologies such as authentication systems in logging tools require cybersecurity.

Cybersecurity technology plays a major role in the concept of digital financial services and digital financial inclusion, attaching a data security documentation from the ITU-T Focus Group Digital Financial Services, an organization of the United Nations, in the next chapter.

Transformational agendas have created revolutions in countries. This led to changes in the organizational structures, and the implementation of new technologies have brought about process changes and technological reform mandates.

ICT revolutions have led to the adoption of new ideologies by teams that create innovative applications.

Accessibility can be classified as the driver of new ideologies and change management. It can be further divided into two categories: socio-economic reforms and sustainable development.

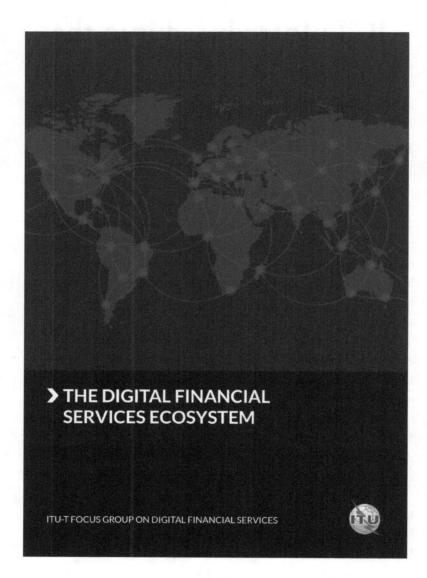

> THE DIGITAL FINANCIAL
SERVICES ECOSYSTEM

ITU-T FOCUS GROUP ON DIGITAL FINANCIAL SERVICES

International   Telecommunication   Union

ITU-T   FG-DFS

TELECOMMUNICATION
STANDARDIZATION SECTOR
OF ITU

(05/2016)

ITU-T Focus Group Digital Financial Services

The Digital Financial Services Ecosystem

Focus Group Technical Report

International Telecommunication Union: An Introduction

The International Telecommunication Union (ITU) is a specialized agency of the United Nations that operates in the field of telecommunications, information, and communication technologies (ICTs). The ITU Telecommunication Standardization Sector (ITU-T) is a permanent organ of ITU. ITU-T is responsible for studying technical, operating, and tariff questions and issuing recommendations to standardize telecommunications on a worldwide basis.

The procedures for the establishment of focus groups are defined in the recommendation ITU-T A.7. TSAG set up the ITU-T Focus Group Digital Financial Services (FG DFS) in its meeting in June 2014. TSAG is the parent group of FG DFS.

Deliverables of focus groups can take the form of technical reports, specifications, and so on, and the focus groups aim to provide material for consideration by the parent group in its standardization activities. Deliverables of focus groups are not ITU-T recommendations.

ITU 2016

About This Report

This technical report was written by the following authors, contributors, and reviewers:

Carol Coye Benson, Charles Niehaus, Mina Mashayekhi, Nils Clotteau, Trevor Zimmer, Bruno Antunes, Yury Grin, Peter Potgieser, Quang Nguyen, Graham Wright, Nathalie Feingold, Ashwini Sathnur, Johan Bosini, Jeremy Leach, Oksana Smirnova, and Evgeniy Bondarenko.

If you would like to provide any additional information, please contact Vijay Mauree at tsbfgdfs@itu.int

Contents

Executive Summary

This report defines the Digital Financial Services (DFS) ecosystem and describes the players and their roles within the ecosystem. These players include *users* (consumers, businesses, government agencies, and non-profit groups) who have needs for digital and interoperable financial products and services; *providers* (banks, other licensed financial institutions, and non-banks) who supply those products and services through digital means; the financial, technical, and other *infrastructure* that makes them possible; and governmental *policies, laws, and regulations* that enable them to be delivered in an accessible, affordable, and safe manner.

The report recognizes the goal of reaching "digital liquidity"—a state wherein consumers and businesses are content to leave their funds in digital form, therefore reducing the burden of the "cash-in and cash-out" process. Various high-level challenges and issues in the ecosystem are acknowledged in the report: Many of these are the subject of more detailed reports produced by the focus group. Finally, the report looks at the many products and services that comprise the DFS ecosystem.

1   Introduction

The ITU DFS Focus Group is charged with describing the overall ecosystem of DFS, identifying the players within that ecosystem, and identifying the key elements necessary to make the ecosystem develop in such a manner that it encourages and enables financial inclusion policies.

1.1   What Is the DFS Ecosystem?

The DFS ecosystem consists of users (consumers, businesses, government agencies, and non-profit groups), who have needs for digital and interoperable financial products and services; the providers (banks, other licensed financial institutions, and non-banks), who supply those products and services through digital means; the financial, technical, and other infrastructure that makes them possible; and governmental policies, laws, and regulations that enable them to be delivered in an accessible, affordable, and safe manner.

The DFS ecosystem aims to support all people and enterprises within a country and support national goals, including financial inclusion, economic health, and the stability and integrity of financial systems.

1.2   The Goal of Digital Financial Services

The goal of financial services made available via digital means is to contribute to the reduction of poverty and deliver on the recognized benefits of financial inclusion in developing countries.

Financial inclusion means the sustainable provision of affordable financial services that bring the poor into the formal economy. An inclusive system includes a range of financial services that provide opportunities for accessing and moving funds, growing capital, and reducing risk. Such services may be provided by banks and other traditional financial services organizations or by non-bank providers.

Many people have pointed out that financial inclusion is a means rather than an end. Financial inclusion contributes to the development goals of poverty reduction, economic growth and jobs, greater food security and agricultural production, and women's economic empowerment and health protection.

The financial inclusion benefits of a DFS ecosystem include the following:

- **Safety and Security:** Poor people are able to store and manage value without needing to protect cash as a physical asset.
- **Speed and Transparency:** Given the liquidity and transactional anonymity of cash, cash payments are subject to delay, "leakage" (payments that do not reach the recipient in full), and "ghost" (fake) recipients. This is particularly true in the context of government payments. By moving to digital payments, the traceability of the payment process is improved through more stringent identification procedures, direct transfers that skip current intermediate hands, digital record-keeping, and more immediate funds transfer.
- **Increased Flexibility:** Many poor people, particularly those in rural areas, receive part of their annual income through domestic and international remittances. They may also reach out to their social networks in times of need to obtain additional funds. At times, these monies do not arrive at all or do not arrive in time. The transfer can be costly, and it is not clear to the payers that their funds will be directed to the proper purpose. DFS can reduce costs and increase the coverage of remittances transfers, making remittances of small amounts viable. Moreover, digital financial systems can enable remitters to direct funds directly to savings, health, education fees, or other types of targeted accounts and ensure funds are being spent as intended. The increased flexibility of digital systems also allows the poor to pay for goods and services on

lay-away, pay-as-you-go, or through other payment options that more closely match their ability to pay.

- **Savings Incentives:** Digital technology facilitates access and interfaces to saving products. Furthermore, digital payments create the opportunity to embed poor people in a system of automatic deposits, scheduled text reminders, and positive default options that help people overcome psychological barriers to saving. Moreover, digital technologies can make available data analytics on users' financial lives and therefore increase the willingness to save.

- **Credit Histories:** Electronic payments create records, allowing transaction histories that can support borrowing by poor consumers and merchants.

- **Women's Empowerment:** Evidence suggests that digital financial remittances (domestic and international) empower women within their households. The digital nature of the payment enables the recipient to keep financial transactions private, even within a family.

Most typically, DFS are seen within the context of one country, using accounts denominated in that country's currency, and institutions that are regulated by national regulators. But these services increasingly intersect, on many levels, with those of other countries, on both a regional and a global basis. It is a goal in the development of DFS to make sure that services are able, as and when appropriate, to efficiently and safely connect to and integrate with services in other countries.

1.3   The Digital Financial Ecosystem and Its Components

The actors and services that constitute a DFS Ecosystem depend on two fundamental support structures: an enabling environment and a solid level of infrastructure readiness. Figure 5.1 represents the description of the entire end-to-end architectural features that are required for the building of the ecosystem of the DFS.

- **Infrastructure Readiness**—consists of payments systems available for transaction between and among end-users, including consumers, merchants, businesses, and governments. These payments systems

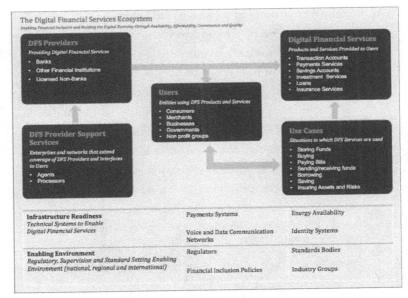

Figure 5.1 Digital Financial Services Ecosystem

may be public, semi-public, or private; they may be "closed-loop" or "open-loop." Security of payments systems is a requirement of infrastructure readiness. In addition, a certain degree of payments system interoperability among participants in payments is a necessary component of infrastructure readiness.

- Voice and data communication networks support financial messaging among end-users and providers. Certain levels of communication network quality and security are a necessary component of infrastructure readiness.
  - Energy availability is sufficient to support the users of a digital financial ecosystems.
  - Identity systems are capable of identifying end-users and their providers, and authentication systems are capable of recognizing and validating these identities. Identity systems may be national IDs, sectorial IDs (e.g., financial industry identifiers, bank account numbers, mobile phone numbers), or private sector IDs (e.g., WeChat or PayPal identifiers) and are also important in the DFS ecosystem. Some national IDs in particular are biometrically enabled; this is expected to become a significant part of the ecosystem.

- **Enabling Environment** consists of the following:
  - ○ Implementation of laws and regulations, including those laws that include the basic permissions given to financial institutions in the countries; the authority of financial regulators, and regulation and permissions given to non-bank financial services providers. Similar law and regulation around the role of ICT providers and the authority of telecom regulators may be relevant in a country. Some countries may have specific legislations enabling or constraining eMoney. Laws and regulations pertaining to competition and consumer protection are also significant in their impact on the development of the ecosystem.
  - ○ National policies, particularly with respect to financial inclusion.
  - ○ Standards setting bodies and their standards. These bodies may be specific to one industry group (e.g., EMV) or be more broadly applicable (e.g., ITU, ISO, ANSI).
  - ○ Industry groups that act on behalf of large numbers of individual providers—these are most typically industry-specific (e.g., GSMA, Mobey Forum).
  - ○ NGOs and development organizations working to implement DFS ecosystems (e.g., World Bank, CGAP, UNCAD, and the Bill & Melinda Gates Foundation).

The ecosystem also includes, of course, the many consumers, businesses, and governments involved in the use and provision of DFS. This includes the following entities:

- **Users**—this term is used to include all entities that are users of DFS: consumers, merchants, billers, and other payments acceptors; businesses; governments; and nonprofit agencies. These groups can be collectively thought of as "consumers" of DFS.
- **DFS Providers**—this term is used to include all entities that provide DFS to end-users. It includes both the so-called traditional financial services providers (banks, savings institutions, credit unions, and other chartered financial institutions) and other entities, which may include eMoney operators, postal authorities, and a variety of different commercial providers. These other entities are collectively referred

to here as "non-bank providers." The ability of non-banks to act as DFS providers is constrained by national laws and regulations.

- **DFS Providers Support Services**—this term is used to include all entities that provide services to DFS providers. This includes processors, platform providers, and a wide range of software and hardware (e.g., terminals, ATMs) providers. It also includes agents (who may work on behalf of either bank providers or non-bank providers) who are an important component of the DFS ecosystem.

A note on providers: Any given company or organization active in the DFS ecosystem may play multiple roles. For example, an eMoney operator may be both a provider of data and voice services (in "infrastructure readiness") and a direct DFS provider. A card network may be both a provider of a payment system (again, in "infrastructure readiness") and a DFS support service provider.

The end-users and providers of the digital financial ecosystem meet in the provision and use of the actual *DFS*: These services then support the *use cases* within the ecosystem.

DFS may include the following:

- **Transaction Accounts** for the safekeeping of funds: These include both bank accounts and eMoney accounts. Deposits into a bank account create a liability by the bank to the account holder: This liability is often guaranteed or insured by government agencies. Deposits into an eMoney account (by definition from a non-bank provider) create a liability by the provider to the account holder: This liability is usually covered by a regulatory requirement that the provider hold funds, in aggregate, in an escrow or trust account at a bank. eMoney accounts and bank accounts are both considered "Transaction Accounts" within the ecosystem.
- **Payments Services:** They provide the end-users the ability to transfer money into or out of an account: This may be done through a variety of different payments systems and providers. Remittances, transfers, merchant payments, bill payments, and so on are all examples of payments. Payments may be domestic or cross-border. For the purpose of this report, we concentrate on digital payments,

which are payments initiated or processed electronically rather than by paper. Bank ACH and RTGS systems, eMoney transfers, and card payments are considered to be digital payments.

- **Savings Accounts:** These are designed to allow consumers to set aside some funds in storage for intended later use. Savings products typically offer some type of interest rate or return. Some savings services have shared, club-like characteristics.
- **Investment Services** are designed to allow consumers or businesses to invest with the aim of securing future financial returns.
- **Loans:** This term encompasses a broad variety of services that extend credit to consumers or businesses. Microfinance, secured and unsecured lending, and mortgage financing are all included in this category.
- **Insurance Services:** This term encompasses a broad variety of services to enable consumers and businesses to protect lives and assets.

Use Cases are situations where consumers and businesses require or consume DFS. A given use case may be satisfied by a variety of different DFS. Many use cases have two end-users; for example, in a "paying bills" use case, both the consumer or business paying the bill, and the biller receiving the payment, are involved. Use cases include the following:

- **Storing Funds**—the need to keep funds safely.
- **Paying for Purchases**—the ability to pay for goods and services purchased: The purchase may be done either locally ("face to face") or remotely.
- **Paying Bills**—the ability to pay for services delivered upon receipt of a bill.
- **Sending or Receiving Funds**—the ability to transfer funds to and receive funds from another end-user (person or business).
- **Borrowing**—the ability to borrow funds for later repayment.
- **Saving and Investing**—the ability to have a short-term liquid to semiliquid investment such as an eMoney account, savings account, or group savings, and the ability to invest funds for future financial returns.
- **Insuring Assets**—the ability to insure lives or assets.
- **Trading**—the ability to participate in international trade through the use of DFS.

1.4   The Evolution of the DFS Ecosystem

The root of the development of the DFS ecosystem is, of course, the rapid and widespread adoption of mobile phones. In virtually every country, this has created a base of capability among consumers, including the most poor consumers and small businesses, to transact and interact electronically. The equally rapid spread of the phenomenon of "mobile top-ups" — the ability to convert cash into airtime minutes—created a second important capability in the eventual development of what is known as eMoney.

In a well-known story, some developing countries allowed non-bank providers, often mobile network operators (MNOs), to create transaction accounts allowing their subscribers to store funds in these accounts and make transfers to other subscribers. These became "closed-loop" payments systems, and the general model is often referred to as a "non-bank-led model." The primary weakness of these systems has been a lack of interoperability: The subscriber to one system cannot pay to the subscriber of another system.

In other countries, regulators chose to support banks as the primary providers of DFS. In these countries, either existing or newly formed payments networks, available to banks and, in some cases, their partners, form the platforms on which these providers can deliver services to their customers. In several countries, regulators have tried to achieve financial inclusion goals by broadening the set of providers who are allowed to access these payments networks, either directly or through bank partners. These systems are generally considered to be "open-loop" systems, and the general model is often referred to as a "bank-led model." The primary weakness of the "bank-led" model has been adoption among the poor of the country.

Both models, when looked at from a financial inclusion perspective, share a common problem: Funds put into these transaction accounts are not left there but are rather withdrawn to cash almost immediately. An ecosystem dependent on networks of agents, branches, or ATMs to support "cash-out and cash-in" has obvious problems with costs and the management of infrastructure.

The idea of a post-cash state of "digital liquidity" has obvious appeal. Consumers and businesses would leave their funds in electronic form, rather than "cashing out." What would it take for the ecosystem to evolve to this state? Four principle drivers are commonly recognized. Each of these is the subject of more detailed reports from this ITU Focus Group.

- The delivery of "bulk payments" —either G2P (Government to Person) or B2P (Business to Person) into digital wallets (transaction accounts managed by mobile devices) is seen as a critical enabler for consumer adoption of wallets. Bulk payments can not only deliver funds immediately into digital wallets but can also improve the odds that the recipient will get their full intended payment.

- The enablement of merchant services or, more broadly stated, payments acceptors to receive payments out of digital wallets is seen as the most important feature in eventually reducing dependency on "cash-out." People will be more willing to leave funds in a digital wallet if they are able to use these funds as they currently use cash.

- The development of interoperability among providers of transaction accounts is seen as the key capability to enable "ubiquity"— the ability of any one payer (consumer or government or business) to make payment to any receiver, regardless of who is providing the transaction account for that receiver.

- The delivery of additional financial services, such as savings, lending, and investing, through connection to the digital wallet is seen as the key to realizing many of the longer-term objectives of financial inclusion. Consumers and small merchants who are able to safely save and invest money, and borrow to support short- or long-term needs, are more able to stabilize their financial lives and avoid many of the perils experienced in an all-cash economy.

Just as different countries have chosen different early models for DFS (many developed at a grassroots level), countries will also see different pathways to a full deployment of these services. However, we expect to see increased regional or global coordination on policy issues connected with the ecosystem, which may lead to more convergence among countries on supported models and systems.

1.5   Issues and Challenges in the Ecosystem

Not surprisingly, regulators, providers, and the wide range of parties working to implement and enable the DFS ecosystem are dealing with complex issues. Many of these issues are the subject of separate reports from this ITU Focus Group.

- Who should be permitted to be a provider of DFS, and how should this be regulated? Although this is often thought of as a question of banks versus telecommunications companies, in fact many other types of entities are currently supplying or can potentially supply DFS through various means, including social networks. Should regulation be done based on function or type of provider? What is the regulatory capacity within a country to support additional provider categories?
- What are the business models for DFS among providers? Are the business models used in pilot and early launch sufficient to support a scaled implementation of the ecosystem? Are transactional costs well understood? What types of systemic controls used in legacy service models (e.g., interchange in bank payments systems, or retail price regulation in telecommunications services) are appropriate for new services? Are business models dependent on elements of the ecosystem that may disappear over time—such as "cash-out" fees? What is the role of government as a provider of DFS? As a user of the same services? Are the necessary infrastructure investments being made?
- How should national (or industry-specific) identity systems be used by the DFS ecosystem? Will emerging biometric-based identity systems be sufficient to change the current costs of "KYC" (know your customer) processes for providers?
- How will consumers be protected from abuse by providers and/or other end-users? How should this be regulated? How can consumer protection be accomplished without adding costs to the ecosystem that make services too expensive for consumers to use?
- How will the ecosystem balance the need to protect consumer (and merchant) data privacy needs against the value the data may have in helping to support the costs of the ecosystem?

- How should DFS providers—and their support services providers—manage the risks in the ecosystem? How should "best practices" be communicated and assimilated? How should this be regulated?
- What standards of quality of service should providers be held to? How should this be defined and regulated?
- Rapidly changing technology presents risks and opportunities within the ecosystem. This includes changes in mobile handset capability, vendor platform capabilities, and changes in the underlying communications networks. How can providers, support services providers, and regulators understand the impact of these changing technologies?
- How aligned to regional or global standards should DFS providers be?
- Should DFS providers be required to use regional or global standards for payments messaging? Is this necessary in order to conduct cross-border financial services in an efficient and safe manner? How should this be regulated?
- How should the digital financial ecosystem work to improve financial literacy among consumers and small businesses? To what extent is this a government function or a commercial function?

An important overarching issue in the development of the DFS ecosystem is the need to invest in and manage two sides of the ecosystem at once. Practically, this means supporting initiatives to load electronic money into consumer transaction accounts—principally through bulk, or G2P payments and initiatives to enable consumers to spend this money in electronic form rather than cashing out—principally through the enablement of merchant electronic payment acceptance. Neither initiative can be successful without the other: Consumers who accept electronic money will simply "cash-out" if they can't spend it electronically, thus perpetuating the costly cash management problem of agents. Merchants, on the other hand, won't accept electronic payments unless there is a significant number of consumers who are ready to make them. Solving this problem is sometimes referred to as reaching a state of "digital liquidity." Figure 5.2 represents the description of the use case requirements and pictorial flowchart mechanism for enabling and creating the transaction

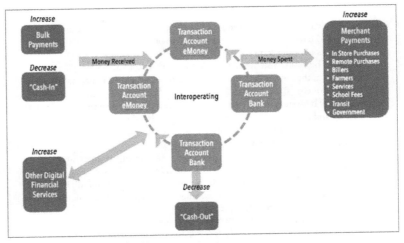

Figure 5.2 Reaching digital liquidity

of a digital payment during the purchase of an item in the market supply value chain.

2   Products, Services, and Use Cases

2.1   Requirements

Products and services in the digital financial ecosystem are delivered to users to satisfy their needs in the use cases described previously. All of these systems have to meet the requirements of users. Across the spectrum of consumers, businesses, governments, and other entities that use the digital financial ecosystem, the following high-level user requirements are noted.[1]

2.2   Products and Services

Figure 5.3 represents the description of the terminologies and the definitions of the concepts and ideologies that are featured in the theories during the procedures of building the products and services of the DFS and financial inclusion, while utilizing the information and communication technologies.

---

[1]Bill & Melinda Gates Foundation, Level One Project Guide, 2015.

Secure: People need to trust that money held in a digital transaction account is secure and have assurance that money will go only to the designated recipient, with a record of the transaction.

Affordable: The cost to use the system must be very low. To actually replace the use of cash, the cost to the consumer (as well as to the merchants) will need to be close to zero.

Convenient: The system needs to have better accessibility and be easy for users to sign up and use. Many poor people do not have the identity documents usually required to create financial accounts. The system has to be understood by prospective users with limited or no mediation.

Open: The system needs to be able to reach many (ideally all) counterparties for both making and receiving payments. It should not require special, costly, or time-delayed accommodations. It should make it easy for an individual to integrate into multiple financial systems of the country, including those systems utilized by higher-income earners.

Robust: A digital payment system needs to have high performance and must be capable of satisfying user's needs. It needs to be available for use as needed, like cash. As the number of participants (and their usage volume) grows, system availability should remain high enough to handle peak volumes without interruption in services provided.

Figure 5.3 Products and services

2.2.1   Transaction Accounts

Users, including consumers and merchants, have a requirement to store their funds safely. Today, poor consumers and merchants in developing countries do this largely through holding cash. Alternatives include eMoney wallets provided by both non-bank providers and bank accounts. eMoney wallets have been successful in reaching consumers who have not been able to access transaction accounts from bank providers.

2.2.1.1   What Is eMoney?

Before defining the details of the respective products and services features and functionality, it is useful to understand the broader eMoney platform in the context of where it sits in traditional banking ecosystem. There is often a misconception as to where the value actually resides: Is it similar to physical cash in a wallet or closer to electronic cash in a savings account at a financial institution?

- eMoney is a liability of an eMoney provider (sometimes called Issuer), who records a value against a transaction account ledger they keep for the depositor. Deposits can either be made in cash (typically through an agent) or by receipt of a transfer from another consumer, business, or government entity. The eMoney provider typically uses a software platform from a support services provider to account for the ledger balances.

- Regulation requires the eMoney provider keep the entire value of accounts on their ledger on deposit in an aggregated account at one or more commercial banks. This account is often structured as a trust account. The total in the trust account must always equal the total on the eMoney provider's ledgers of customer balances.

eMoney, in one sense, is similar to money in a bank account, in that it represents a liability of the provider to the account holder. Funds held in banks, of course, are typically protected by some form of government insurance, and banks are allowed to lend or otherwise invest a certain amount of balances held in an account. Funds held with an eMoney provider do not typically have the same types of government insurance, but they are "100 percent reserved" through the funds held in deposit at the trust bank or banks.

2.2.1.2 *Description*
A transaction account is an individual account hosted by a DFS services provider (either an MNO, a bank or some other type of provider permitted to do so by regulation). The term "digital wallet" or "mobile wallet" is generally used to refer to a transaction account that is primarily accessed through a mobile device. A transaction account typically allows deposits and withdrawals in cash (discussed later in "cash-in and cash-out"). Prepaid cards may act as transaction accounts in some markets.

2.2.1.3 *Attributes*
Product attributes for transaction accounts accessed through digital devices include the following:

- Safety (access is through unique PIN code)
- Security (actual store of value ledger is registered on a secure platform accessed through the handset)

- Speed (balances and transaction occur in real time)
- Convenience (accessed through the handset)

2.2.1.4   Business Model

The various providers of transaction accounts have different business models. Notably, eMoney wallets and bank accounts have different business models. Banks have a multidimensional business model based, for example, on intermediation of deposits, cross-selling of loans, and several fees. For example, banks are sometimes allowed to charge a monthly service fee for banking accounts (depending on regulation, product, and segment). An MNO acting as an eMoney wallet provider may have a simpler business model, which will often depend on fees generated through cash-in and cash-out transactions. An eMoney wallet provider's business model may also vary depending on whether the MNO is directly licensed or set up as a subsidiary.

The business model is often driven by the lead institutions' broader strategy:

- MNO-led models: A large percentage of airtime in the emerging markets is prepaid and sold through third parties. MNOs thus have a challenge as attrition rates are high and cost of distribution via the third-party airtime resellers is also high. An eMoney account adds an element of "stickiness" to the client relationship, solving a portion of the attrition challenge. An eMoney account also enables the MNO to sell prepaid airtime directly to the consumer, thus eliminating the commission cost associated with distribution through third parties. Traditionally, MNO-led models have been seen as a loss leader for their core businesses. As the industry matures, although depending on its structure and licensing arrangements, regulation and management pressures may lead to standalone business units to be formed within the MNOs. eMoney businesses are therefore becoming standalone profit centers within the MNOs.
- Bank-led models: In some markets, regulation has forced bank-led models. From a business perspective, eMoney platforms and associated accounts are often seen by banks as a low-cost hosting

alternative to traditional banking platforms introducing a low-cost product, "lite" solution, to reach the lower end of the market. eMoney accounts are thus seen as an onboarding product by banks.

Independent models: Independents do not traditionally have the brand and reach that MNOs and banks have and have generally approached the market by using mobile to compete with existing paper-based remittance products at a domestic level. They vary in their business model with some offering accounts and others offering over-the-counter (OCT) money transfer services.

2.2.1.5 *Best Practices*

The following areas have been identified as best practices for digital wallet providers[2]:

- Overcoming logistics and delivery challenges—a lack of infrastructure creates logistical challenges for agent and cash management. Leveraging local partnerships, flexible agent financing, and smarter transactional data analysis are enabling providers to address these challenges.
- Identifying and communicating a compelling value proposition—understanding the nuances of how consumers earn, save, and spend their money can help providers develop a relevant value proposition.
- Creating a user-friendly service and accessible interface—as poor customers tend to have lower financial and technical literacy levels, the service will require a user-friendly interface to enable access. While technologies such as IVR can be useful for reaching illiterate users, greater investment in customer education and increased "touch points" are also proving successful as a means of onboarding customers.
- Finding solutions to the lack of formal identification documents— the absence of compulsory population registration and identification is a common barrier to widespread adoption of digital wallets.

---

[2]GSMA, "e-Money in Rural Areas," 2014.

In most markets, regulation plays an important role; solutions such as tiered KYC and adjusting acceptable KYC documentation can help providers facilitate customer adoption and increase the success of financial inclusion initiatives.

- Current offerings and the future of money accounts—current offerings are primarily limited to a temporary store of value and OCT transactions. As the industry matures, deeper and richer offerings beyond a basic store of value for the eMoney account will emerge. Money accounts may potentially become closer to traditional bank accounts but could also have nimble and bespoke product features that banks have traditionally struggled with.

2.2.1.6   *The CICO Problem: Cash-In and Cash-Out Services*

Cash-in and cash-out (CICO) services represent both a critical enabling element of the DFS ecosystem and a current and long-term problem. As an enabling element, CICO is simply necessary in order to deal with consumers who have cash on hand and want to use a digital wallet to send the funds to someone else and to deal with consumers who receive electronic credit into a wallet and need to get cash to use. CICO often goes hand in hand with a Person to Person (P2P) transfer, where consumers would cash-in (CI) at an agent, perform a P2P transfer, and the recipient performs a cash-out (CO) at another agent.

The short-term problem—often quite severe—is dealing with the liquidity and cash management needs of agents, who at any point in time may have too much or not enough cash on hand to support their business. The long-term problem is an economic one: Since many providers build their part of their digital wallet business model on cash-out fees, a successful transition to "digital liquidity" (when a consumer leaves funds in their wallet to be spent electronically) would present serious challenges to this model.

In some countries, "Super Agents" or "Master Agents" may be responsible for a set of underlying agents. There are a variety of models within countries for agent regulation. In some countries, agents (or their "Master Agents") are exclusive to one provider (bank or non-bank). In other countries, agents are permitted by providers (and/or required by regulation) to support multiple providers. This can be accomplished either by the agent enrolling and registering with each provider independently, or by some type of agent interoperability system, possibly provided by the "Master Agent."

Note that in bank-led models, the CICO function is provided primarily by bank branches and by ATMs. Bank-led models deployed to accomplish goals of financial inclusion normally have agent relationships (and economics) that are similar to those of non-banks.

2.2.1.7   Description

A cash-in transaction requires an eMoney account holder to deposit physical cash at a participating agent of their joint scheme. The agent accepts the cash and transfers e-money to the user's eMoney account (i.e., mPesa account at an mPesa agent). A cash-out transaction requires an eMoney account holder to transfer e-money to a participating agent of their joint scheme. The agent receives the e-value and gives the user physical cash.

CICO transactions therefore don't change the total monetary value held on the eMoney provider's platform (and in the bank trust account); they merely change the ownership of eMoney and physical cash between users and agents of the providers.

Attributes of successful CICO models include: safety (all transactions are PIN based), speed (transaction takes place in real time), and convenience (agent distribution is widespread).

2.2.1.8   Business Model

To attract funds into the system depositing users do not need to pay to deposit. Similarly, agents are incentivized by DFS providers to attract funds into the system by earning commissions for cash-in transactions. To withdraw funds from the system, users pay a fee to withdraw cash. Agents also earn commissions for cash-out transactions. Therefore, the business model leans toward users performing cash-out transactions funding the bulk of the ecosystem.

2.2.1.9   Best Practices

Agent management is a critical success factor for the CICO service to perform optimally. Factors that contribute to a successful agent management include the following, which should aim to expand and consolidate efficient, effective, and trusted networks:

- Agent selection and recruitment
- Agent training
- Agent incentives
- Agent liquidity management
- Agent monitoring

2.2.1.10   *Current Offering and the Future of CICO*

- Current business models incentivize CO transactions, thus countering the long-term ambition to keep cash digital.
- Agents have potential working capital constraints when making trade-off decisions between allocating cash to eMoney (for cash-in transactions), keeping physical cash on hand (for cash-out transactions), and allocating the cash to purchase other goods that may turn a higher profit leading to liquidity challenges.
- Providers have aggressively competed on rolling out agent networks, and pricing competition has led to reduction in agent commissions.
- Competition and pricing pressure may lead to situations where agents may not see value in CICO transactions.
- As bulk payment matures the funding side may potentially replace a large portion of the current OCT cash-in transactions.
- As merchant payment matures and a merchant payment business model is defined the cash-out transactions may be cannibalized. There may however be arbitrage issues where agents could encourage cash-out transactions (and exchange the cash for goods) instead of merchant payment transactions as they earn a higher margin from cash-out than they might from merchant payments.

2.2.2   Payments Services

A wide range of payments services are provided to users of the DFS ecosystem. These services are almost all bi-party; that is, there is both a sender and a receiver of funds, and the transaction account of each party needs to support the payments processes necessary to accommodate these transactions.

Note that two areas of payments services, which are of particular importance to the development of the DFS, are described in separate reports from this Focus Group and therefore are not described in detail in this report. These areas are **merchant payments** (including all forms of commercial payments acceptance such as bill payment) and **bulk payments**.

2.2.2.1   *Domestic Transfers (Remittances)*

A domestic digital funds transfer is the exchange of funds from one user to another through a DFS provider using electronic means, including a mobile handset, to either initiate and/or complete the transaction.

A digital funds transfer competes with traditional money transfers services, which are performed in various regulated and unregulated ways. The regulated environment includes licensed money transfer companies, such as banks and post offices, and the unregulated environment includes both unstructured and structured personal cash-transport services. In some parts of the world, these structured services are referred to as "hawala." The advent of eMoney accounts has enabled efficiencies to be gained against these traditional streams as cash can be digitized through an agent of a trusted service provider, sent instantly across vast distances, and immediately cashed out at another agent of the trusted service provider. Product attributes include security (all transfers are PIN based, initiated by the sender) and convenience (transactions happen in real time).

The business model of the domestic transfer provider is a "send" fee to be paid by the sending consumer. The business model is tightly coupled to that of the underlying digital wallet and CICO services.

Cash-to-mobile transfers are often referred to as "over the counter" (OTC). In this transfer, a user sends funds from an agent (by giving the agent cash) that are then credited to a recipient mobile subscriber. Much like mobile-to-mobile transfers, receivers are alerted of an incoming funds transfer through their mobile handset. The transaction happens in real time with the recipient eMoney account receiving the credit.

Mobile-to-Cash Transfers: Value is sent from an eMoney account to a recipient who is not on the same network. The receiver would be alerted via SMS on its handset of an incoming funds transfer. Funds have to be collected from an agent of the sender. Much like cash-to-mobile transfers discussed previously, the mobile-to-cash transfers rely on the receiving party's ability to have easier access to the relevant agents.

Interoperable Mobile-to-Mobile Transfers: As the industry matures, interoperability between different service providers is becoming a reality. In this transaction, the sender sends eMoney from their eMoney account to a recipient who could have an eMoney account at another service provider or potentially a bank. The business model for these transfers is typically based on the sender paying for the transaction, and the receiver paying a fee if they cash out or perform further transactions. This is offset by fees paid to agents by providers. Interoperability business models are being developed. Although the trend seems to point to sender paying models, these can range from copying an ATM carriage fee (sender pays) model, to a surcharge (sender pays) model, to an interchange model where the receiving institution pays the sending institution and the sender or receiver does not pay any extra for off-us transactions.

Best practices include having the transactions credited to the receiver in real time. An emerging best practice is account verification, so that the sender sees a real-time message—"Do you mean to send money to [Name]?"—before finalizing the transaction: This reduces errors and resulting inquiries and disputes.

2.2.2.2   International Transfers (Remittances)

A transfer is made from a consumer in one country to a consumer in another country. As these transactions are normally cross-currency as well, the transaction requires someone—either the sending or receiving party, or the providers who are serving them—to effect the currency exchange.

Traditional models for sending cross-border remittances include money transfer services, many of which are specific to certain corridors (pairs of countries); banks, and structured cash transfer, that is, hawala-style services. The advent of eMoney accounts has resulted in a number of experiments with using the e-wallets to either receive or, in some cases, send cross-border remittances.

Many DFS service providers have built partnerships with traditional international remittance operators such as Western Union and Money-Gram. This model requires the sender to transfer from a developed market through the provider's existing process, with the recipient receiving their funds directly into their eMoney account. The recipient would then cash out through their local agent.

Cross-border remittances have started between regional DFS operators with agreements being announced in West and East Africa. The nature of these agreements are still bilateral and either occur in a cross border "on-us" environment (i.e., from a provider's company in one country to the same provider's company in a second country) or in an "off-us" environment.

The cross-border environment faces many regulatory challenges, including issues such as exchange controls licensing, varying AML and KYC policies, and central bank policies around clearing and settlement.

Product attributes include convenience, immediacy, and potentially lower costs.

2.2.3   Bulk Payments

This refers to payments made to multiple recipients. Typically, these are government payments (benefits, cash transfers, salaries), donor payments, or payroll payments. Bulk payments are a critical enabling component of the DFS ecosystem and are the subject of a separate report from this ITU Focus Group.

2.2.4   Merchant Payments

This refers to payments made to merchants or other payments acceptors (such as billers or governments) for purchases. These payments may be made in person (POS or "proximity payments") or remotely (eCommerce or "mobile" payments). Merchant payments are a critical enabling component of the DFS ecosystem and are the subject of a separate report from this ITU Focus Group.

2.2.5   Savings Accounts

2.2.5.1   Description

Digital savings products can broadly be defined into two product groups: individual savings and group savings.

2.2.5.1.1   Individual Savings

Individual savings products tend to satisfy two overlapping needs on the part of consumers. One is for a return (interest) on money that is being held. The other is segregation of funds (away from the "everyday spend" of the transaction account) for short-term money management. Saved funds may be either earmarked for specific purposes (school funds, the purchase of a bicycle) or be for more general needs (saving for emergencies).

Products in this space may create a partition in the eMoney account to keep a certain amount of liquid funds for daily use and the specific needs are stored in less liquid "partitions" to be released separately when the consumer requires it. Other providers may create separate savings accounts. Some providers create bundled products such as savings and credit combined where the savings sometimes forms part of the security for the loan product.

2.2.5.1.2   Group Savings

DFS providers have designed products to facilitate group savings schemes. These schemes copy many "club savings" products popular in the developed world, where a group of people contribute to a "pool" and that pool is distributed by lottery or formula. In the digital world, the group's cash is stored on the eMoney platform, which will release the funds to an individual once a set of conditions are met (e.g., three individual PINs are entered) to release funds and individuals in the group receive SMS notification when transactions happen.

From a business case perspective, DFS providers see savings products as a tool to build balances in the eMoney ecosystem and ultimately earn revenue from transactions generated off the digital wallets.

Current mobile savings products are still in the early phase of the evolution of DFS. Inception transactions have been nuanced toward OCT money transfer transactions, but indications are that savings products are starting to gain traction.

The advent of interest-bearing products and sophisticated technology enabling deferred savings products will potentially drive the uptake of mobile savings accounts. A very important regulatory decision will be to consider whether or not eMoney issuers will be able to lend against balances kept in digital wallets.

2.2.6   Loans

2.2.6.1   Description

2.2.6.1.1   Secured Loans

A form of secured loans that is common across emerging markets is Airtime Credit. Service providers give users access to airtime (typically a negative balance on the account) to be paid back when they top up airtime again. The "loan" is thus for airtime and not redeemable for cash. The security is any future airtime purchase and risk models are based on airtime-purchase behavior.

More recently, cash loans are being offered by DFS providers through banking partnerships. In these models, there is often a joint savings and credit account, and the loan is secured against a user's savings. As the models mature they evolve to unsecured lending products. MShwari in Kenya is potentially the most publicized example of this, which is a joint venture between Safaricom and Commercial Bank of Africa (CBA).

2.2.6.1.2   Unsecured Loans

Unsecured loans have been launched more recently in a variety of markets, offering customers access to credit with no direct recourse for nonpayment. Typically, the loan provider will score customers using alternative data sourced from the MNO directly or through other means.

The credit decisions are based on data gathered from entities that collect mobile user data through smartphone apps to build risk models or using MNO GSM and eMoney account data to build dynamic risk models to lend to unbanked customers into their eMoney account. In this model, interfaces can be, for example, USSD to ensure inclusion, and all loans have a risk-based pricing methodology that rewards good repayment with lower prices and bigger loan amounts. Loans are advanced to key participants in the eMoney ecosystem: agents, merchant, and consumers.

2.2.6.1.3 Merchant Loans

An important part of the emerging DFS ecosystem is the provision of credit to small and medium merchants—many of whom have not had previous access to formal credit. Often, these loans are based on information the provider has from seeing the flow of sales transactions handled through the provider. In some instances, the revenue from loans is sufficient to enable very low cost payments transaction fees to the merchant.

2.2.6.2 Attributes

In emerging markets, the providers are often not solving a price problem but rather an access and distribution problem, as the majority of the population is excluded from the traditional lending sectors. DFS allows these segments access to convenient and simple products. Successful products have the attributes of convenience (products are accessed through the handset; no need for branch visits and paperwork) and accessibility (loans paid to eMoney account and for immediate use).

2.2.6.3 Business Model

Different business models exist.

2.2.6.3.1 Direct to Consumer

In this case, a lender will approach customers directly, gather information, and make a credit risk assessment to lend or not. Distribution is often a problem in this model, and the cost of processing and verifying information is important. The provider is not incentivized to process small loan sizes. In addition, as this is stand-alone, there is no integration with the eMoney account for collections translating to significantly higher risk, which typically reduces the provider from being able to take scale risk.

2.2.6.3.2 Two-Way Partnerships

In this model, a lender partners with a DFS provider as a distribution partner to leverage the data and eMoney ecosystem. The DFS provider provides the user and the lender the credit scoring, administration, needed regulatory approvals, and, importantly, the capital. The network is looking for a value-added service to drive eMoney liquidity and transactions; the lender is looking for distribution at a low cost. Typically, the lender will share revenue, profit, or fees with the eMoney service provider to remain aligned.

2.2.6.3.3   *Three-Way Partnerships or Service Providers*

In this scenario, a third-party expert will approach an MNO and provide insights into their data that can be used to build a credit scorecard and intelligence. With this, they would then approach a bank to provide the financial services products. The financial service provider will then share profits or fees with both the eMoney service provider and the third-party provider. The challenge with this model is getting the three parties to agree on a common objective and approach to execution of transfers.

2.2.6.4   *Best Practices*

Best practices are still being established in this space, with many iterations outside of these examples being tried and tested in Southeast Asia, Africa, and Latin America. As with all examples, the most likely to succeed and drive real value and scale will be those operating in collaboration with the MNO, the lender, and the regulator.

2.2.6.5   *Microfinance*

Microfinance is a specialized form of lending with a long history (predating eMoney accounts). Although an important part of the ecosystem, it remains relatively distinct from the eMoney account and the emerging services built from that. There is an important intersection in the use of digital wallets where microfinance providers disburse loans and/or collect payments from loans. Microfinance providers have traditionally had many challenges in disbursement and, more often, in the collection of repayments of loans. eMoney accounts potentially solve some of these pain points, but to date have not garnered momentum outside of the key DFS markets. Indications are that MFIs have refined their collection models and only migrate to integrations with DFS once there is a certain level of DFS ubiquity in a market. There is criticism leveled against microfinance that it is used more for consumption than investment and that it could cause moral hazard leading to oversupply of lending to non-creditworthy clients and, therefore, to over-indebtedness. The provision of microfinance through the DFS ecosystem could potentially amplify this effect. Still, there are needs for financial services that are adequately addressed through microfinance services, especially since they evolved from narrower microcredit services, and this positive effect is also augmented by the DFS ecosystem. This debate underlines the importance of an adequate regulatory and institutional framework for DFS.[3]

2.2.6.6   *International Trade*

The participation in international trade through the use of DFS will not be thoroughly analyzed in the context of this report. Nevertheless, it is relevant to mention how the combined use of several DFS methods facilitates engaging in international trade and thereby promotes access to trade-related development benefits.

For example, in China the e-commerce company Alibaba opted to establish its own e-payment system, which soon expanded to banking, investment, and clearing house for cross-border merchandise trade. The company developed a network of affiliated financial entities that enabled business-to-consumer services. One of these entities, Alipay, had in 2013 approximately 300 million users who were using its online and mobile payment services. This underlines how DFS can provide the right ecosystem for the provision of financial services. It also enabled crowdfunding initiatives by facilitating contributions from a large number of people. Alibaba's platform allowed e-commerce activities by integrating consumers, manufacturers, custom clearing, transport, and several financial services such as credit, foreign exchange, and insurance.[4]

DFS also facilitates the role of international trade in supporting rural development by reducing physical and economic barriers to financial inclusion. Small farmers in rural areas benefit greatly from enhanced

---

[3]Adapted from UNCTAD, 2014, Impact of Access to Financial Services, Including by Highlighting Remittances on Development: Economic Empowerment of Women and Youth and from UNCTAD, Forthcoming, Access to Financial Services and Digital Economy for Sustainable Development.

[4]Adapted from UNCTAD, 2014, Report of the Expert Meeting on the Impact of Access to Financial Services, Including by Highlighting Remittances on Development; Economic Empowerment of Women and Youth.

connectivity to access financial services, to reach clients and providers, and to obtain updated price information on their products. Access to mobile savings and credit services can allow small farmers to purchase the necessary inputs for their agricultural activities. In addition, mobile credit and insurance services can enable their connection to markets and ultimately alleviate poverty in rural areas.

The introduction of a mobile wallet system in Nigeria increased agricultural productivity in the country, which was previously declining. Small farmers depend on subsidized fertilizer, but often this would not reach beneficiaries. This was addressed by the introduction of mobile technology to transfer fertilizer subsidies directly to farmers, removing the government from the role of procuring and distributing fertilizer. The transfer system relies on a database with more than 10.5 million farmers who are subsidy recipients, which allows them to have access to formal or regulated financial services. The system is expanding for digital identification systems and biometric signatures, increasing rural financial inclusion.[5]

While growing e-commerce creates significant opportunities, lack of security and trust remain a barrier to international trade transactions in the DFS ecosystem. Online fraud and data breaches require adequate legal and regulatory measures, including aligning laws for e-transactions; streamlining consumer protection policies, data protection, and cybercrime laws; strengthening the capacity of policy makers and enforcement authorities; and enhancing the awareness of consumers and companies.[6] The focus area on fraud on this report will develop some of these issues.

2.2.7   Investment Services

2.2.7.1   *Current and Future Investment Products*
Investments (defined as investments into financial products such as stocks, unit trusts, ETFs, etc.) in the DFS space have to date not gained much traction. Some DFS operators are starting to investigate medium- to long-term savings plans linked to money market accounts, but very few have implemented anything.

---

[5]Adapted from the World Bank (2016), *World Development Report.*
[6]Adapted from UNCTAD (2015), *Cyberlaws and Regulations for Enhancing E-commerce.*

Some of the contributing factors to the immaturity of this product offering is potentially a combination of the demand- and supply-side factors, these include:

- Lack of surplus funds for investments at the bottom of pyramid
- Lack of an investment for retirement culture
- Lack of understanding of financial products
- Oversophisticated investment industry
- Cost and fee structures in the investment industry
- Rouge investment advisors
- Lack of regulation in emerging markets
- Limited product offerings in emerging markets for low-value investments
- Limited liquidity in emerging market stock exchanges

As the industry matures and a deeper offering develops investments will potentially emerge as a tool to gaining greater financial health. In particular, the use of various crowdfunding platforms to raise funds for smaller merchants is an area that will be interesting to watch.

2.2.8   Insurance Services

2.2.8.1   *Description*

Mobile insurance is insurance whose sale and/or administration and payment is facilitated by a mobile phone. Insurance products are aimed at protecting individuals or families from a variety of risks such as illness, death, crop failures, and accidents. The growth in mobile handsets and associated distribution benefits accompanying them have enabled insurance firms to design applicable micro-insurance products and reach customers at the bottom of the pyramid.

Products currently focus on health (such as hospital plans) and life (death cover). Interesting agro-insurance products that protect small-scale farmers against drought and excessive rainfalls have also been developed.

Premium collection models vary with some MNOs using eMoney to collect premiums and others deducting premiums from customers' purchased airtime. In some instances, insurance is provided as a reward for purchasing a specific amount of airtime, and, in others, insurance is being offered as part of a loyalty value proposition.

At the end of 2014, the GSMA reported that there were 100 live mobile insurance services globally, and as of June 2014, the industry had issued 17 million policies and was growing fast.

2.2.8.2 Attributes
Product attributes for mobile insurance include:

- Scale (or at least the potential for significant scale through mobile)
- Typically low-value simple products (reflecting the low-touch model)
- Convenience (access through the mobile infrastructure)

2.2.8.3 Business Model
The business model for mobile micro-insurance products is similar to the traditional value chain and broken down as follows:

- Reinsurer, Insurer (Risk Carrier): Designs appropriate products and pricing based on market and risk assessment and takes a share of risk and premium to cover claims as well as profit margin.
- Administrator/Technical Service Provider: Earns commission or administration fee and in some cases a share of profit for claims processing.
- Aggregator, for example, MNO: Mainly performs sales and client reach functions, earns commission and, depending on commercial agreements, a share of profit.

2.2.8.4 Best Practices
The following seven points illustrate some of the factors key to the success of these offerings[7]:

- A captive, large market and a strong brand
- Simplified product design and processes

---

[7]GSMA, "Seven Keys to Success in Mobile Insurance," 2015.

- Focus on both quality and quantity
- Offer of multiple types of insurance cover to customers
- Building loyalty models, then upselling with suitable payment mechanisms
- Mixing digital sales with high-touch sales
- Enabling regulatory environment

CHAPTER 6 .

The Various Steps of the Processes of Building Cybersecure Applications

The various processes of cybersecurity, such as digitization, innovations, and strategy development, in organizations begins with concept development. A conceptualization development is first defined and established.

Next arises product proposal building. So, a proposal creation team is formed. Later, product requirements are defined, followed by setting criteria to be used in the processes of designing, development, testing, and final deployment of product.

Teams are formed around these stages, and members are constantly motivated to make positive contributions.

Providing incentives to workers, awarding best performance, and appreciating the teams lead to constructive work delivery.

The ideologies and theories on cybersecurity requires dissemination to the public, as it is a newly created methodology in new sectors such as digital financial services.

Building or enhancing innovative skills in teams would boost positive outcomes of the project. Innovations would drill down to the development results, if the implementation of innovative ideas becomes a mandate in the program.

Thus, development teams hold the key to the delivery of the innovations!

CHAPTER 7

The Types of Risks that Emerge With the Concept of Fraud

New ideologies and innovations bring forth both opportunities and risks. Some of the risks arise out of privacy implications because of the rise in the use and rapid development of digital technologies. Illegal access or misuse of any product or service is called fraud. The various types of fraud are listed as follows:

A) Online theft of data
B) Accessing an individual's secure and private data
C) Hacking important information
D) Tampering with secure information
E) Manipulating secure information

Fraudulent activities could be performed by technological methodologies.

Hackers write software codes for illegally gaining access into computer servers containing important data.

By certain investigation mechanisms in the Internet methodologies and also by detecting third-party entries into the data security firewalls of websites, fraudulent activities could be detected.

Cryptography is a scientific and technological subject and concept of data security. Technological tools are built on these ideologies. Various programming models are devised to enable the functionalities of cryptography security algorithms, and solutions are built for desktop and mobile applications.

Data privacy is a concept of securing private information of an individual or an organization. This concept can be utilized to create applications of programs in software languages.

Consumer protection is protecting the rights of individuals who are consumers. This could also be built by requirements such as gathering, designing, developing, testing, and deploying data in a variety of application suites and frameworks.

Database modules and programs are the most important sections of cryptography, data privacy, and consumer protection. Database management languages are built with cryptography modules to verify the existence of fraudulent activities and also to prevent and mitigate these fraudulent activities.

CHAPTER 8

Consumer Protection and Financial Inclusion

Cybersecurity is a mandatory requirement in the digital financial inclusion platform. Elimination of the occurrences of fraudulent activities during funds transfers is primarily achieved by cybersecurity technologies. Blockchain technology has created a revolution in digital financial inclusion strategies. Digital financial services first originated in international trade. Cybersecurity is an important and vital concept for the success of digital financial inclusion. Here, consumer protection plays an important role.

Data privacy and cryptography whose ideologies have been described earlier are key components in the cybersecurity technology used for digital financial services and blockchain.

CHAPTER 9

Solar Flares and Quantum Neural Networks

Besides digital financial inclusion, artificial intelligence (AI) is also a component of the digital technologies frontier. AI is the latest revolution in the field of digitalization. Human intelligence quotient and thinking capacity are built into AI programming.

Cybersecurity algorithms and solutions are also built into neural networks and deep learning in order to decipher possibilities of occurrences of data theft.

Neural networks and cybersecurity modules are built utilizing the tools of programming languages such as MATLAB.

DENSE NEUTRINOS—Neutrino Oscillations in Dense Medium: Probing Particle Physics Together with Astrophysics and Cosmology

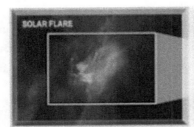

By Ashwini Sathnur
Capacity Development Expert in United Nations Development Programme

Solar flare is a gust of solar eruption wind from the surface of the sun. This solar wind travels from the surface of the sun in the form of a beam outwards.

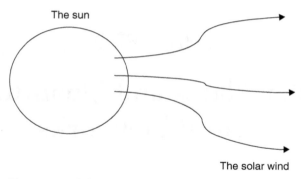

Figure 9.1 Solar wind

These winds rush outwards from the sun to the various planets and moves outwards toward the regions outside the solar system—away from Uranus, Neptune.

As and when the winds approach the planets, the planets' temperatures rises. Along with the temperature rise, several other effects can be observed.

This wind arises due to excessive nuclear fusion, giving rise to excessive generation of photons and particles. This leads to a massive outburst and movement of cosmic particles from the sun's surface toward both the Earth and other planets.

Large amounts of hydrogen nuclear fusion results in large generation of helium with energy particles.

The effects of solar flares are observed especially in populated human settlements such as urban regions and cities. This is due to the fact that cities are the direct recipients of sunlight and the heat and warmth from the sun rays as well as solar flares.

$$4 \text{ Hydrogen} \rightarrow \text{Helium} + \text{Cosmic particles} + \text{Photons}$$

The greater the amount of hydrogen, the greater the amount of cosmic particles generated. These cosmic particles emerge from the sun and are pushed to move as the solar wind with the photon energy blows toward the Earth's surface.

A certain region on the sun's surface generates solar flare. This is directed as a beam onto the Earth. This beam strikes the Earth at a certain region that is facing the solar wind. During the later decades of the 20th century, the solar wind had created a massive effect on Quebec.

Solar wind affects radio communication and telecommunications and causes electricity and power loss. In the dark ages, this was not observed because there was no electricity. But when these occur in contemporary times, the effects are immediately visible.

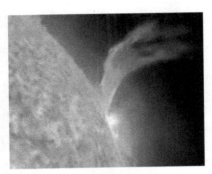

Figure 9.2 Solar flare gushing outwards from the sun's surface

Neuron is the building block of the human brain. It aims to perform the cognitive functioning of the human body. Every neuron comprises cosmic particles and protons that contain certain chemical compounds and elements.

This proton is tuned to be in harmony with the protons in the cosmos. Protons in the neurons oscillate with a certain frequency along with the cosmic proton particles.

In other words, the human brain is composed of cosmic particles which includes protons which are muons.

The entire cosmos is made up of oscillating proton particles that travel the universe in proton beams. Human body is surrounded by cosmic particles because it is surrounded by the cosmos!

And these cosmic particles constantly collide with the human body—every second!

In order to maintain peace and harmony and balance, the quantity of cosmic particles within the human body must oscillate and balance against the external oscillating cosmic particles, that is, the universe and its cosmic particles.

If there is a slight variation between the quantity of particles in the body and the quantity of the particles in the cosmos, then there could be a possibility of imbalance. If there is imbalance, it adversely affects human health and gives rise to diseases, including diseases such as mental illnesses, Alzheimer's disease, and so on.

Proton beams arise from the solar wind and enter into the Earth's atmosphere, which results in the generation of muons in the Earth's atmosphere. These muons then enter the human body and adversely affect the health of the individuals.

Protons + atmosphere → muons

Muons + human body → imbalance between

A) the quantity of the human's cosmic particles and
B) the universe's cosmic particles

Imbalances as depicted above → Human ill-health such as Alzheimer's

A product based on the above-mentioned observations is the "Solar flares, Astrophysics, Brain-on-chip and Quantum Neural Network Learning/Response Generation Mobile Application!"

Changes that keep occurring in atmospheric conditions due to sun's solar flares affect adversely the health of human beings and a variety of mammals.

These health changes in the mammals, including human beings, in the current decade has led to a variety of changes in the atmosphere, in water, on land, and so on. These changes affect the neurological functioning of human brain, which could lead to disorders such as Parkinson's disease and Alzheimer's disease. The current technology used in life-long neurological disorders is neural networks.

It has been found that this change modifies the functioning of nuclei in the neuron in the human brain. This brings about changes in the motion/movement of nuclei. The size of the neuron is in dimensions of nano. Such changes in each and every neuron would lead to a change in the movement/or distortion in the human brain as a whole. This is apparent when all the neurons, which are millions in count, are aggregated into one unit—the human brain.

Hence, this distortion causes the malfunctioning of human brain.

Brief Description of the Solution and Its Innovative Elements (max 400 words)

Since the problem deals with nano dimensions, quantum mechanics comes into the picture. Thus, quantum mechanics concept is embedded within the neural systems.

Quantum mechanics dealing with neural systems come under the purview of the subject quantum neural networks.

These effects on the human brain are captured in the organ-on-chip biomedical bioengineering devices. On the brain chip, these innovative ideas and functionalities are inscribed and manufactured. This device is then launched in a mission to the International Space Station, where the experiment on the device, that is, the brain-organ-on-chip, is carried out. Then, the various effects of solar flares—as described in the experiment above—are tested on the biomedical bioengineering device. The inferences are captured from the device and then the neural networks algorithm creates a solution with the utilization of an AI and machine learning product application that is executed on the device. This AI solution is a product that is tested and validated on one human being. This test is performed by that human's exposure to the solar flares. Upon successfully implementing this solution on that one individual, it is provided as a must and required solution to all the human beings residing on the Earth. In other words, the solution is provided and marketed to the entire human community or the society!

The solution to the problem is a quantum neural network learning/response generation mobile application. It is created to enable the disabled person suffering from Parkinson's or Alzheimer's disease. And it helps the disabled person to understand the stimulus that he or she is looking at by his or her visual system. Once the stimulus is fetched from the disabled person, via his or her visual system (which he or she is looking at), it is processed in the biological neural network processing system within the mobile application.

And an output object is created that can be defined as a response to the stimulus. From the mobile application, this response is displayed to the disabled person. And then this response action is carried out by the disabled person.

Also a quantum neural network learning tutorial is played in an animation format in the mobile application that explains the disabled person about the disability, neural networks, quantum mechanics and neural networks, and the usage manual of the mobile application.

Evidence of Impact/Effectiveness in an Applied Development Context
(max 250 words; attach additional key information in a separate document if necessary)

This is demonstrated on disabled persons in an institution.

Decisions/Actions Taken to Scale Up Implementation (max 200 words)

Existing methodology is neural networks.

Health changes affecting the human brain scale up the neural networks application to quantum neural networks learning/response generation mobile application.

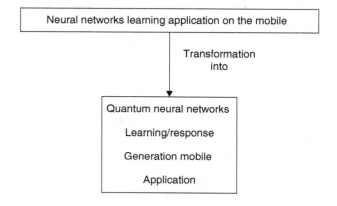

Energy

$$H = T + V$$

where T is the potential energy and V is the kinetic energy.

$$V = \frac{1}{2}mv_{vel}^2 \,; vel = \frac{dx}{dt}$$

$$V = \frac{1}{2}m\left(\frac{dx}{dt}\right)^2$$

$$\text{momentum } p = mv_{vel}$$

$$V = \frac{1}{2}mv_{vel}\left(V_{vel}\right)$$

$$\therefore V = \frac{1}{2}p\frac{dx}{dt}$$

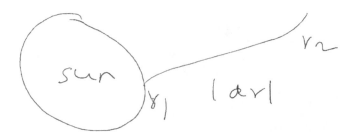

Distance of solar flare

$$= |dr| = r_2 - r_1$$

$$H = T + V$$

$$= \frac{1}{2}m\left(\frac{dx}{dt}\right)^2 + \frac{1}{2}kx^2$$

$$\therefore \frac{dH}{dT} = \frac{d}{dT}\left[\frac{1}{2}m\left(\frac{dx}{dt}\right)^2\right] + \frac{d}{dT}\left[\frac{1}{2}kx^2\right]$$

$$= \frac{1}{2}m\left[\frac{d}{dt}\left(\frac{dx}{dt}\right)^2\right] + \frac{1}{2}k\frac{d}{dT}\left[x^2\right]$$

$$= \frac{1}{2}m\left(\frac{d^2x}{dt^2}\right)^2 + \frac{1}{\cancel{2}}k\,\cancel{2}$$

But $\dfrac{dH}{dT} = 0$

$$\frac{1}{2}m\left(\frac{d^2x}{dt^2}\right)^2 + \frac{1}{2}kx$$

$$\int 0 = \frac{1}{2}m\int\left(\frac{d^2x}{dt^2}\right)^2 + \frac{1}{2}\int kx$$

$$0 = \frac{1}{2}m\left(\frac{d^2x^2}{dt^2}\right) + \frac{1}{2}k\frac{x^2}{2}$$

$$0 = \frac{1}{2}\left[m\left(\frac{d^2x}{dt^2}\right) + kx^2\right]$$

$$\therefore 0 = m\left(\frac{d^2x}{dt^2}\right) + kx$$

$$\therefore m\frac{d^2x}{dt^2} + kx = 0$$

But $x(t) = A\cos(wt + \phi)$

$$\frac{d(x(t))}{dt} = -wA\sin(wt + \phi)$$

$$\frac{d^2x}{dt^2} = -Aw^2\cos(wt + \phi)$$

$$\therefore \frac{dH}{dT} = \frac{1}{2}mA^2w^2\cos^2(wt + \phi) + KA\cos(wt + \phi)$$

$$\downarrow$$

total energy released due to solar flare

Q = mass of hydrogen − mass of helium

Energy of nutran + energy of electron $= \dfrac{dH}{dt}$

$$\frac{dN_e}{dE_e} = p^2(Q - H)^*$$

$$\frac{\sum_{i=1}^{3}|u_{ei}|^2\sqrt{(Q - H)^2} - \text{man of one hydrogen}}{}$$

Quantity of particle $= \sqrt{\dfrac{dN_e}{dE_e}} \Big/ p_e$

Quantity of particles in the cosmos is now greater.

Hence, imbalance in the body $\rightarrow (m_H - m_{He} - H)^2 - m_H^2$
$$= m_{He}(m_{He} - 2m_H)$$
$$\approx m_{He} \gg 1$$

Thus, the quantity is much greater after the occurrence of solar flare, that is, the number of particles now is much greater in the cosmos leading to human imbalance in health.

A brief ideology on the introduction and massive adoption rates of cybersecurity in the areas of digital technologies is for the sole purpose and objective of achieving a mandate of "Eliminating Fraudulent activities"; that is, obliging and approving the requirements of privacy objectives for individual users as well as institutional users.

The era prior to the revolution in digital technologies witnessed huge utilization of the Internet or the World Wide Web.

This widespread application of the Internet gave rise to fraudulent activities such as hacking and breach of privacy of data and information.

This has also created job opportunities for technologists and researchers to develop applications in the field of cybersecurity.

Cybersecurity is required in all the subjects and research areas that deal with the concept of mitigating fraudulent acts and breach of privacy of data/information.

This ideology has led to the introduction of cybersecurity in several subject and research areas. As described in this book, cybersecurity has become integral to successful functioning of systems in digitization, financial inclusion, blockchain, artificial intelligence, and so on. There are many other subjects as well that now need cybersecurity applications more critically.

Thus, we can ultimately say—"Thanks to Cybersecurity for having created tools that ensure safe and secure use of Internet and digital technologies for all users and everywhere in the world!"

About the Author

Educated in the Birla Institute of Technology and Science Pilani, and Indian Institute of Management Kozhikode and Indian Institute of Management Lucknow, *Ashwini Sathnur* joined United Nations Development Programme as capacity development expert. With expertise in strategy planning, project management, supply chain management, software development, programming, and application implementation and testing, she has been recognized in areas such as business process mapping, requirement study, and defining the various specifications for application implementation. Employment opportunities being worked upon include UNDP expert in Capacity Development, UN—Habitat Inclusive Digital Transitions in Cities Working Group member, ITU—T Focus Group Vehicular Multimedia member, ITU—T United 4 Smart Sustainable Cities member, ITU—T Focus Group Digital Fiat Currency member, ITU—T Focus Group Digital Financial Services member, UN Space ISWI member (International Space Weather Initiative), ITU—T Artificial Intelligence Group member, and Knowledge Management in the United Nations.

Index

OTHER TITLES IN OUR BUSINESS LAW
AND CORPORATE RISK MANAGEMENT COLLECTION

John Wood, Econautics Sustainability Institute, *Editor*

- *The History of Economic Thought: A Concise Treatise for Business, Law, and Public* Policy, Volume II: After Keynes, Through the Great Recession and Beyond by Robert Ashford and Stefan Padfield
- *Buyer Beware: The Hidden Cost of Labor in an International Merger and Acquisition* by Elvira Medici and Linda J. Spievack
- *European Employment Law: A Brief Guide to the Essential Elements* by Claire-Michelle Smyth
- *When Business Kills: The Emerging Crime of Corporate Manslaughter* by Sarah Field and Lucy Jones
- *A Freelancer's Guide to Legal Entities* by Alex D. Bennett
- *Corporate Maturity and the "Authentic Company"* by David Jackman
- *Counterintelligence for Corporate Environments, Volume I: How to Protect Information and Business Integrity in the Modern World* by Dylan van Genderen
- *Counterintelligence for Corporate Environments, Volume II: How to Protect Information and Business Integrity in the Modern World* by Dylan van Genderen
- *Contract Law: A Comparison of Civil Law and Common Law Jurisdictions* by Claire-Michelle Smyth and Gatto Marcus
- *Board-Seeker: Your Guidebook and Career Map into the Corporate Boardroom* by Ralph Ward
- *Conversations in Cyberspace* by Giulio D'Agostino
- *Cybersecurity Law: Protect Yourself and Your Customers* by Shimon Brathwaite

Business Expert Press has over 30 collection in business subjects such as finance, marketing strategy, sustainability, public relations, economics, accounting, corporate communications, and many others. For more information about all our collections, please visit www.businessexpertpress.com/collections.

Business Expert Press is actively seeking collection editors as well as authors. For more information about becoming an BEP author or collection editor, please visit http://www. businessexpertpress.com/author

Announcing the Business Expert Press Digital Library

Concise e-books business students need for classroom and research

This book can also be purchased in an e-book collection by your library as

- a one-time purchase,
- that is owned forever,
- allows for simultaneous readers,
- has no restrictions on printing, and
- can be downloaded as PDFs from within the library community.

Our digital library collections are a great solution to beat the rising cost of textbooks. E-books can be loaded into their course management systems or onto students' e-book readers. The **Business Expert Press** digital libraries are very affordable, with no obligation to buy in future years. For more information, please visit **www.businessexpertpress.com/librarians**. To set up a trial in the United States, please email **sales@businessexpertpress.com**.